Books in the Linkers series

Reprinted 2001
First paperback edition 1996
First published 1996 in hardback by A&C Black (Publishers) Limited
37 Soho Square, London W1D 3QZ

ISBN 0-7136-4604-7
A CIP catalogue record for this book is available from the British Library.

Commissioned photographs by Zul Mukhida
Design by Jean Wheeler

Consultants
Grant Jones, Art Adviser, E. Sussex
Ian Punter, Adviser in Design Technology, E. Sussex

Acknowledgements
The publishers would like to thank the children in Reception, Year 1 and Year 2 of
Wallands County Primary School, Lewes who worked so hard to produce the artwork featured in this book,
and Judy Grahame and Annette Bolton who facilitated and guided its production.

Picture acknowledgements: Bridgeman Art Library; Private Collection 20 (left), Stapleton Collection 20/21 (centre),
Private Collection 21 (right), Chapel Studios; 8 (left).

Printed and bound in Italy by L.E.G.O.

Toys

discovered through
Art and Technology

Karen Bryant-Mole

Contents

A & C Black • London

Exploring toys

Toys are usually made from lots of different parts that are assembled, or put together, in a particular way.

Ask a grown-up if you can take apart one of your toys.

How many different pieces make up the toy? Can you see how the pieces fit together? Look for any gears, levers, push-buttons or switches.

Now, see if you can put the toy back together again!

Toys have to be good at the job they are supposed to do.

A car should run smoothly, a teddy should be soft and cuddly and a game should be fun to play.

Look at some toys and decide what makes them good at their job.

3

Board games

You have probably played with board games, like the one below, at home or at school.

Some board games are very easy to play while others have lots of rules and are quite complicated.

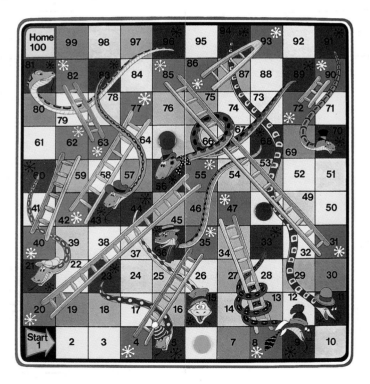

You can design and make your own board game.
How will you play your game?
Will you use playing pieces and dice?

Here are some board games that a group
of children have designed.
Can you see one that is based on the story
of Jack and the Beanstalk?

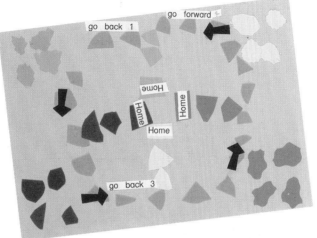

go forward

go back 1

Home
Home
Home
Home

go back 3

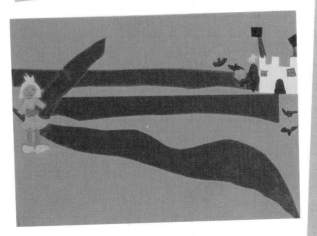

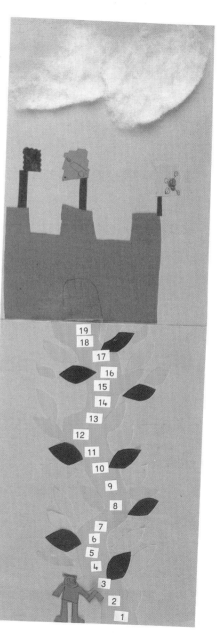

19
18
17
16
15
14
13
12
11
10
9
8
7
6
5
4
3
2
1

Toys that light up

This toy taxi has headlights and a sign that lights up just like a real taxi.

To make a toy that lights up you need to make an electrical circuit, using a battery.

A battery has energy stored up inside it. When the ends of the battery, or terminals, are joined together by wires, the electrical energy flows through the wires.
This is called a circuit.
If a light is included in the circuit, its bulb will light up.

Can you spot the
shining light bulbs in
these toys?

**Never play with ordinary
light bulbs or with plugs and
sockets around your home
or school.**

They are dangerous.

Large toys

This little girl is playing on a wooden horse and wagon. The wagon is big enough for her to climb inside.

You could use big boxes to make your own large toy.
This big box has been made into a washing machine.

These boxes are being made into a bus.
When it is finished, a child will be able to sit in the cab.

This toy did not cost much to make. However, it will be quite difficult to store away neatly.

Can you think of other good or bad points about this toy?

Puppets

There are lots of different types of puppet.

To make a sock puppet, all you need is an old, clean sock and a few odds and ends.

Put your hand into the sock.
Perhaps it makes you think of an animal's head?

When you have decided what you would like your puppet to look like, you can choose materials to help you create that look.

Here are some puppets made by a group of children.
If you take a close look you will see a puppet with eyes
made from buttons.

Jigsaws

Jigsaws are made by cutting pictures into pieces.
To do the jigsaw you have to put the pieces back together again.

You can make a jigsaw by cutting up an old birthday or Christmas card.

Think about who you are going to make the jigsaw for and then find a card with a picture that the person might like.

It is easier to do a jigsaw with a few pieces than one with lots of pieces.

Which of these puzzles do you think a child would like to do? Which would a grown up enjoy?

Pop-up toys

This is a Jack-in-the-box.
The doll is on the end of a spring.

When the lid is closed, the spring is squashed down.
When the lid is opened, the doll springs up.

You could use strips of paper or card to make
a simple spring.

Cut out two long thin strips, both
the same size.
Glue the two strips together.

In turn, fold one strip over the glued
ends and then the other strip.
Then glue the two loose ends together.

Some children have used paper springs to make their own pop-up toys.

They have decorated the boxes in lots of different ways.

Toys that make other toys

Toys that can be used to make things are sometimes called construction toys. This construction toy has been made into a helicopter.

Most construction toys have lots of pieces that can be put together in many different ways.

You can make your own toy. Decide what you want to make, then, before you start building, think about the pieces you will need.

If you want
to make
something
that moves,
you will probably
need some axles and wheels
attached to a base.

If you want to make a toy with
moving parts, you will probably
need some gears
like these.

Here are some ideas
for toys made from
another toy.

Paint patterns

This toy makes swirling paint patterns. The patterns are made by squirting paint onto a piece of spinning card.

There are lots of different ways to make patterns and designs using paint.

You can mix some paint into some bubbly water and lay a sheet of paper over the bubbles.

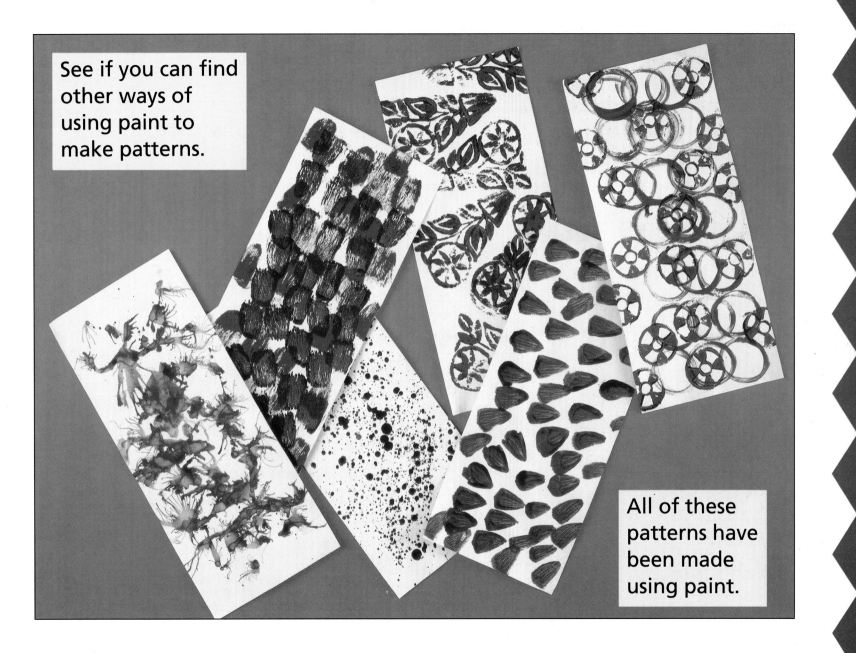

See if you can find other ways of using paint to make patterns.

All of these patterns have been made using paint.

19

Toys in art

Here are some works of art that feature toys.

This painting was made about 400 years ago.
The artist used oil paints on a wooden panel.

The picture above is
a lithograph.
The black lines were
made using a special
type of printing.
The picture was then
coloured in by hand.

The picture below is a modern painting.
The artist used watercolour paints to paint this picture.

Which of these pictures do you like the best?
Why is it your favourite?

Your toy pictures

You can make your own toy pictures,
using some of your favourite toys.

There are lots of different ways
to make your pictures.

This collage has been
made by sticking pieces
of material on to paper.

This picture
of the same
group of toys
has been
painted.

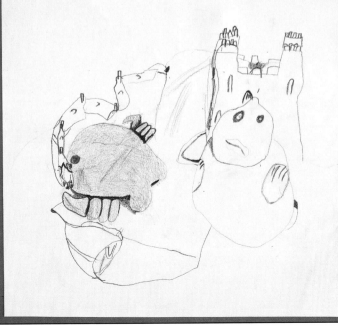

You do not have to use colour in your
pictures, you could use a pencil instead.

Look at this picture. Can you see how
the pencil has been used lightly in some
places and heavily in others?

Why not make a set of pictures like
this yourself?

Glossary

axles rods on which wheels turn

construction to do with building

gears a set of wheels with notches or teeth around the edge that connect together to help a machine work

lever a bar or handle that is used to lift or move things

lithograph a type of printed picture made using special inks and a particular type of stone

plug a way of connecting a piece of electrical equipment to the electrical supply

socket the holes into which a plug is pushed

spring a coil that can be pushed in but will jump back out again when you let go

switch a way to turn equipment on and off

Index

How to use this book

This book takes a familiar topic and focuses on one area of the curriculum: art and technology. The book is intended as a starting point, illustrating one of the many different angles from which a topic can be studied.

It should act as a springboard for further investigation, activity or information seeking.

The following list of books may prove useful.

Further books to read

Series	Title	Author	Publisher
First Technology	Toys and Games	John Williams	Wayland
Knowhow Books	Action Toys	H. Amery	Usborne
	Batteries and Magnets	H. Amery & M.J. McNeil	
Painting and Drawing	Poster Paints	M. Angels Comella	A&C Black
	Watercolours	"	
	Wax Crayons	"	
What Shall I Do Today?	What Shall I Make?	R. Gibson	Usborne
	What Shall I Paint?	"	
	What Shall I Draw?	"	
You and Your Child	Odds and Ends	R. Gibson	Usborne
	Paint Fun	"